Seer of the unseen

The truth beyond the veil

L.Packham

By L. Packham

Seer of the Unseen: The Truth Beyond the Veil

© 2025 by L. Packham

All rights reserved. No part of this book may be reproduced, stored in a retrieval system, or transmitted in any form or by any means—electronic, mechanical, photocopying, recording, or otherwise—without the prior written permission of the publisher, except in the case of brief quotations embodied in critical articles or reviews.

This is a work of nonfiction based on personal experience. Names and identifying details may have been changed to protect the privacy of individuals.

ISBN: 978-1-923511-00-2

Cover design by L. Packham

Edited and formatted with love and intention.

Printed in Australia

First edition, 2025

For Norma,

My grandmother –

The quiet oracle who hears what others cannot.

The world may not have understood your music,

But I did. I always did.

Where they saw confusion, I saw clarity.

Where they whispered doubt, I saw Divinity.

You carry the forgotten songs of the soul,

Melodies that pierce the veil and call us home.

You are the soft strength that walks between worlds,

A keeper of the truth no noise can silence.

May the sound within you rise like a sunrise,

Guiding you gently, powerfully,

Back to the arms of the light.

You were never broken;

You were remembering.

And I will never let the world forget your song.

Table of Contents

The Whispers of Beginnings 1
The Silent Knowing 5
The Moment I Began to Respond 9
Trapped in the Loop 11
Watchers in the Fog 13
The Ones Who Walk Between 15
Faces That Weren't Mine 17
Where No One Hears Your Cries 19
Where Nightmares Bow 21
Master of the Board 23
The Last Flame – Rethinking the Ego 25
The Return of the Infinite One 27
The Lion's Roar 33
The Lioness and Her Cubs 35
The Rise of the Divine Feminine 39
In the Beginning… was the Lie 41
The Matrix – A Construct, Not Creation 43
The Reincarnation Trap – A Beautiful Lie 47
The Great Forgetting 49
The Override Codes 51
The Final Exit 53
Heaven was Never Far 57
The Truth Hidden in the Dark 59
The Mirror and the Flame 61
Final Prayer 63

For the ones who remember.
This book is not for everyone;
it is for the ones who've felt the veil thin around them. For
the ones who have questioned whether what they were told was real.
For the ones who can't quite put it into words – but know,
deep down, that something about this world is wrong.
I'm not here to teach you anything you don't already
know.
I'm here to help you remember.
We are here to remember who we are and to choose freedom.
This is not a book of affirmations.
It is not a guide to enlightenment.
It is a remembering.
A calling.
A return to truth.
Some of what I say may challenge you. Some might
confirm what you've long suspected. Either way, my only
prayer is that these words stir something ancient inside you.
Not because I need you to believe me, but because your
soul is already nodding in recognition.
If you ever felt like you were here for more, like your voice
was meant to protect, to disrupt, to awaken, then this book is
for you.
You are not crazy.
You are not alone.
You are seer of the unseen.
And it's time to remember.

CHAPTER ONE

The Whispers of Beginnings

In the silence before dawn, where the veil between worlds thins and the unseen stirs, there exists a truth, timeless, ever-present and yet often overlooked. It is here that the soul finds its voice, not in the material world, but in the quiet resonance of what is beyond.

It is said the eyes are the windows to the soul, yet the soul does not speak through the eyes alone. It speaks through the stillness, the moments when the world falls away and what remains is the truth we have carried since the beginning of time. For the soul knows no time. It exists outside of it, in the eternal dance of creation.

When I first began my journey, I was much like others. I searched, driven by a deep longing for answers.

But it was not until I stopped searching with my mind and began to listen with my heart that the whispers of truth reached me. They came softly at first, like the rustling of leaves in the wind, a flicker of light, a fleeting thought, a strange knowing that bloomed in the depths of my being. I understood in that moment, that the world as I knew it – the world of illusions and distractions – was not the whole of reality. There was more, far beyond the material. The unseen realms, the spaces between thoughts, the whispers of the Divine, were all around me, waiting for me to open my heart and receive them.

So, I began to walk the path of the seer, not to gain power, but to understand the depths of the mysteries that had eluded me for so long. To see what others could not, and to know what had been forgotten.

But the journey of the seer is not one of ease. It is fraught with challenges, with moments of doubt and fear, for the truth is not always comfortable. The deeper one ventures into the unseen, the more one must confront the shadows that lie within. Yet, it is in these shadows that the greatest revelations are found.

For the truth, as I have come to understand it, is not a singular thing. It is not confined to one path, one tradition, one way of being. The truth is vast like the sky, limitless and ever-changing, it is both ancient and new, hidden in the depths of the soul and yet shining brightly for all to see. If only they knew how to look.

So, I stand here, at the threshold of this book, this sacred journey, not as a teacher, but as a fellow traveller. I offer these words not as answers, but as questions. Not as certainty, but as invitations. For the path of the seer is not one that can be walked alone. We walk it together, each soul a reflection of the divine, each step a dance with the unseen.

May this journey be one of awakening, remembering and opening to the infinite possibilities that lie beyond the veil.

CHAPTER TWO

The Silent Knowing

There comes a point where you stop lying to yourself- Not with dramatic outbursts, but in quiet, private moments when truth finally becomes impossible to ignore. For me, it was a slow accumulation. A pattern I could no longer not see. I'd walk into a room and feel the energy shift. I'd hear someone speak and instinctively know whether it was genuine or hollow. I couldn't explain how I knew. I just did. At first, I tried to brush it off. Told myself I was over thinking. That I was too sensitive. But the accuracy of those feelings kept proving themselves, again and again. My body would tighten before something bad happened. I'd feel uneasy around people who later showed their true colours. I wasn't guessing – I was sensing. Picking up what others couldn't say or didn't want me to notice.

This was the real beginning of clarity.

It didn't feel magical. It felt practical. Like finally hearing the sound of your own footsteps after years of walking through noise. I wasn't imagining things – I was noticing things. Things I'd been trained to ignore.

That "silent knowing" was never really silent. It had been speaking to me for years through my gut, my tension, my insomnia, my frustration. The problem wasn't that I didn't hear it – the problem was I kept overriding it to make others comfortable.

In the early days of my awakening, I would search for answers in the noise – the frantic tapping of fingers on the keyboard, the rustling of pages and the voices of others who claim to know. Yet, all I found was confusion, a maze of well-meaning advice and half-truths. Nothing truly resonated with the deepest part of me, the part that had been whispering for years unseen, unheard.

I began to understand that the mind is not the seat of truth. It is a tool, yes, but one that must be wielded with awareness. The heart, however, is the gateway. When I let go of my need to control and simply allowed myself to feel, to receive, to be present in each moment, the truth came to me – not in words, but in the deep knowing that emanated from my core.

The first time this happened, I was sitting at the beach, the water calm and still. As I gazed into the depths, something stirred within me a flash of understanding – a glimpse of the interconnectedness of all things – washed over me. It was not a thought but a feeling, an experience of oneness with everything around me. I felt the pulse of life beneath the surface, the subtle energy that ties all things together.

I closed my eyes for a moment; I was no longer just a person sitting by the ocean, I *was* the ocean, the earth, the sky. I was the whisper of the wind, the movement of the trees. I was part of the greater whole, a piece of the cosmic puzzle, and I knew deep in my bones, that this was not an illusion; it was the deepest reality.

It was in these moments that I realised the truth; the unseen is not separate from us; it is us. We are part of the fabric of existence, woven into the same cloth as the stars, the trees, the mountains. The answers I sought were not external but within, they were hidden in silence, waiting for me to listen. The path ahead is not always easy. There will be times when silence feels deafening; when the unseen seems distant and unreachable. But even in those moments, the knowing is still there, waiting to be rediscovered.

The universe is always speaking in whispers and sighs. The question is not whether it speaks, but whether we are willing to listen.

CHAPTER THREE

The Moment I Began to Respond

There was a restlessness I couldn't name. On the surface, life moved forward – quietly, uneventfully. But something beneath it all was shifting. I didn't understand it at the time, but a quiet unravelling had begun. A question would rise without warning. A strange energy would fill the room. A flicker in the mirror that felt like someone – something – was looking back at me.

The first time it happened, I had no idea. I hadn't read about it. Didn't expect it; it just happened.

I woke up in the middle of the night, and my whole body was tingling- buzzing, almost vibrating. It wasn't like pins and needles. It was deeper. Like my whole being was charged with electricity.

I opened my eyes.

And then I felt it – something pulling me upward. At first, I thought I was dreaming, but when I looked down, I saw myself still lying there in my bed. My body was asleep – but I wasn't in it.

That's when it hit me.

I was outside of myself.

Fully conscious. Aware. Floating higher, being pulled toward the ceiling like there was no gravity. It was slow but strong. I passed right through the roof – straight out of the house.

And then I freaked out.

The fear snapped me back like a slingshot. One second, I was out in the night sky, and the next – I was back in my body. Eyes wide open. Heart racing. Sitting straight up in bed, looking around in shock.

It didn't feel like a dream.

It felt more real than real.

After that, I couldn't deny it anymore. There was no way this world was all there was. That moment changed everything! I knew that what we see with our eyes is only the smallest piece of what's really going on.

There are layers to this place.

And I had just been pulled through one.

CHAPTER FOUR

Trapped in the Loop

Not long after that, it started happening more often – but differently. More disturbing.

I'd wake up – or at least, I think I did – with a heavy pressure on my chest. I couldn't move. Couldn't speak. I'd try to yell, try to scream, but nothing would come out. Just silence and panic. There was always a presence there. Sometimes it felt crouched in the corner. Other times, standing tall by the door. I couldn't see a face, but I knew I was being watched. I could see them even through my eyelids, like shadows swimming along the ceiling moving unnaturally. I'd force myself to move. Try to run. My legs wouldn't work right. Like moving through mud. I'd stumble, fall, crawl. And my eyesight distorted, then I'd "wake up".

Only I hadn't.

Same room. Same pressure. Same presence. Over and over. I'd think I escaped and then find myself back at the start. Caught in a loop. Sometimes I was blind. Other times the walls twisted and pulsed like I was walking through a nightmare version of my home.

Every time, I'd wake up feeling like I'd been in a war.

Drained. Shaky. Like I'd been running all night. And I had.

It wasn't just sleep paralysis. I knew it was more.

Something was trying to get in.

Or maybe trying to pull me out.

Each time, it got stronger. And each time, I got closer to something I didn't understand.

CHAPTER FIVE

Watchers in the Fog

Then came the night I broke through again. Everything was grey. Not dark, exactly, but dull. Foggy. Like someone had taken the world and drained all the colour and life out of it. My house was there. My street was there. The trees. But none of it felt right. Everything was off – like a dream made from memory, not the real thing.

But I was flying again.

Just like before, I was outside myself. Weightless. Drifting above the neighbourhood. I wasn't scared at first. I felt calm. Free. I even stopped on a rooftop to rest.

Then everything changed.

A sudden fear ran through me. No noise. No warning. Just instinct. I looked across the sky and saw them.

Three Figures.

They were massive. Rising above the tree line. Not human. Not close. Their eyes glowed gold, and their bodies were insect-like – hard to explain, like shadows that didn't follow the rules of this world. They didn't speak, but I felt them.

They sensed me.

And in that instant, I knew I wasn't supposed to be there. Unarmed and unprotected, shining like a lighthouse throughout the astral plain.

I flew home as fast as I could, heart pounding, every part of me screaming to get back. But when I reached my house, I couldn't get back in. I hovered just outside my body, stuck between worlds. I could see myself asleep in bed.

And then I saw one of them again.

Just standing there. Watching through the window. Still. Silent. Golden eyes burning through the glass.

The fear yanked me back.

I snapped into my body, gasping, heart thudding in my ears. I was awake. Fully back. But the presence didn't leave. I could still feel it. Like it had followed me. Like it had marked me. That was the moment I understood. This world isn't all there is. And some things – some beings – watch behind the veil, waiting for the moment you drift too far.

CHAPTER SIX

The Ones Who Walk Between

Some of them look like shadows. But not like the ones on Walls — more like air shaped into people. A ripple. A bubble. A distortion moving where nothing should move. You can see right through them, yet somehow still see them. Their outline. Their movement. The way spaces around them bend slightly, like heat on glass. They walk. Sometimes slowly, like they're lost. Other times direct — like they've been sent. Not all of them are parasitic. Some are just stuck. I've seen them in my house. It's like seeing into a parallel reality: some don't even realise they're dead. They walk like they're still living. Following old routines. Wandering loops. They don't look at you — until you see them. Then they freeze, unsure or scared. And in that moment, you feel their grief. The confusion. Like they were yanked from life too fast and never found their way out. Forever roaming in the astral…

But the others — they are not lost. They're the Watchers. Sent to monitor awakenings. To observe those pulling away from the system. I started to question everything. That's when they came closer. I'd feel it – before I'd see it. Like a pressure around me. My body would go on alert, even if my mind hadn't caught up yet. And then I'd spot it. Just a few steps away. A shape. A walking silhouette. No eyes. No face. Just a presence that wasn't mine. Studying. Waiting. They weren't here to help. They were sent to gather. To distract. To trigger fear and slow down the light trying to break through. But once you see them, they lose power. You start to feel when the veil thins. You start to know when you're not alone, even if no one else can see it. I call it out. I say, I see you. And if they don't belong in my space I send them away. Because this is my vessel. My home. My path. And no invisible being – lost or sent – has any right to walk beside me unless it comes in truth.

CHAPTER SEVEN

Faces That Weren't Mine

It usually happens right before sleep. In that quiet space where your body starts to drift, but your mind's still awake. Not every night. Not even predictably. But when it does, you know it. You see it.

Flashes.

Faces that aren't yours. Not from memory. Not from dreams. Just – there. Split-second images, too fast to hold, but enough to rattle something deep inside. Sometimes monstrous. Sometimes beautiful. Sometimes it's a loved one. Other times a stranger. But no matter what face they wear, I always feel it – it's not them. It's something using their shape, their voice.

They know.

They know your family. They know what makes your heart ache. What you long for. What you fear.

And they use it.

One night, it was a family member. Her voice gentle. Loving. Saying my name. I turned to face her in the dream, only to find her eyes weren't her own. They were hollow.

Black. Watching. Feeding. Another time it was a man I'd never met, warm and safe, telling me everything I'd ever wanted to hear. Then he changed. His smile stretched too wide. His face began to peel like paper. Underneath, something sinister. Cold. Parasitic. They don't need your body to get in. They slip into your mind. Into your dreams. Wearing masks. Sometimes it's just images – quick, surreal, and violent. A child crying in a dark hallway. A hand reaching through a mirror. Fire where your home should be. Just enough to shake your peace. To siphon energy. To make you carry fear into your waking day. Other times, they use desire. They feed you what you think you want, only to twist it at the last second. They study your wounds. Your losses. They know your soft spots, and they press on them with precision. If you've never experienced it, it's hard to explain. But if you have – you know.

CHAPTER EIGHT

Where No One Hears Your Cries

There's a place beyond pain. Beyond sadness. Beyond all Things; it's the fear of madness. There were days I thought I was losing my mind. Not in the way people joke about when they forget their keys.

I mean *really* losing it.

Hearing things no one else could hear. Sensing things crawling through the veil while everyone else sipped their morning coffee and talked about the weather.

I stayed quiet about it for a long time. Because the moment you say, "I see things" or "I feel things that aren't there," they call you crazy.

They suggest trauma, hallucinations or schizophrenia.

They want to label you before they'll listen.

So, I played the part.

Smiled when I was screaming inside.

Laughed when my skin was crawling.

Held conversation while entire dimensions pulled at me from every corner of the room.

But it was real.

It was always real.

And the fear of going mad wasn't because I didn't trust myself. I didn't trust the system because I knew – I *knew* if I let it show, they'd try to shut it down. They'd medicate it, shame it, gaslight it. And I couldn't let that happen.

So, I learned to walk through spiritual warfare in silence. To nod politely while my soul was under siege. To tuck my knowing into journals and tears. There's a special kind of strength in pretending you're sane when your entire world is falling through the cracks. But I did it. For years.

And madness?

Madness was the price they threatened me with if I dared to remember who I was. But I walked through that fire. And what they called madness, I now call clarity.

CHAPTER NINE

Where Nightmares Bow

One particular night, it started like a dream – but it wasn't. It was a mirror world, a warped reflection, a realm that tried to mimic mine. Everything looked familiar... but beneath the surface, something slithered. It had cloaked itself as me. It copied my movements, my voice, my energy- thinking it would pass unnoticed. But you can't mimic the spark of the Divine. I felt its presence straight away. I screamed, "Who are you?" and in that moment, the illusion shattered. It began to twist, distort – no longer able to hold its stolen skin. I watched it unravel – astral parasite in disguise, weak and exposed. It hissed and shrieked as I dragged it out – out of my dream, out of my space, out of me; I stood tall, unafraid and stood my ground. Claimed my sovereignty. It tried to rush me; one turned into two. A swarm of shadows, a final attempt. But I didn't flinch. Instead, I charged back; I felt a rage that was not chaos, but clarity. A fury born of truth. A holy, surging light that built in my chest, my arms, my hands – I was going to ignite,

A star.

A supernova.

And they knew it.

I felt the surge of energy vibrate through me like lightning – and just as I burst with the Divine fire, they fled, thrown back to the pit they came from, scorched by what I am.

In that instant, I woke up. Not slowly – instantly. My hands tingled. My arms vibrated with power. And I lay there, pulsing with electricity, knowing I would never be the same.

CHAPTER TEN

Master of the Board

I didn't choose to share this, not because it's dark, not to make you uncomfortable. People want awakening to be soft. Light-filled. Beautiful.

And sometimes it is.

But not at first.

Real awakening drags you through the underworld of your soul. It makes you face your fears. That's what changes everything.

Not power. Not revenge. Not escape.

Love.

Love for myself. Love for truth. Love for the Divine that never left me, that lives through me.

It's like chess.

You don't win without setbacks.

You don't learn without risk.

And sometimes, you lose a few pieces of yourself along the way. But every move teaches you.

CHAPTER ELEVEN

The Last Flame – Rethinking the Ego

The spiritual community often speaks of the ego as the enemy – a shadow to transcend, a weakness to dissolve or even a parasite to be exorcised. "Death to the ego," they chant, as if it's the only way to reach enlightenment. But that's only one side of the truth.

I've lived another side.

In my darkest moments when entities whispered lies to break me and when even the voices of the world tried to drown out my own – my ego roared. It said no when I was tempted to say yes to the end. It said get up when I lay crumpled and broken. It said you're better than this when every external voice screamed otherwise.

How could that force be evil?

How could something that refuses to let me die be anything but sacred?

The ego, when imbalanced, can absolutely cause destruction. It can become inflated with pride, arrogance, self-importance. But that's not the ego I speak of. I speak of the tempered ego – the one forged in the fire of survival and anchored in truth. The ego that stands beside the soul, not above it.

The spiritual world often worships passivity as purity. But I've learned that sometimes stillness is surrender – not to peace but to defeat.

There were moments in my life when that calm would have killed me. What saved me wasn't "detachment," it was fire.

It was rage turned righteous.

It was ego – balanced, fierce and clear.

It reminded me that I am not what happened to me. I am not my trauma. I am not the labels they tried to place on me. I am a warrior. A seer. A lion-hearted force. And sometimes, the ego is the last man standing when everything else has been taken.

So, no, I will not kill my ego.

I will honour it.

I will walk beside it.

I will let it rise when I need to remember who I am.

Because in the silent betrayal, in the chaos of abuse, in the blackness of the spiritual attack – "Hold your head high. Get back up. We are not done." And it was right. We are not done. We are just beginning.

CHAPTER TWELVE

The Return of the Infinite One

For so long, I searched outside of myself.

I begged the skies for answers, looked to teachers, gurus, prayed through tears and clawed through lifetimes of pain for a glimpse of who I truly was beneath the masks they gave me.

And then, in the quiet – when there was no more war to fight, no more illusions to entertain... I remembered.

Not through words.

Not through visions.

But through being.

I saw it in geometric pulses – tiny hexagons, tessellating like a living lattice across reality. They were not random. They were light codes, living intelligence embedded into the architecture of creation. They weren't decorations – they were reminders. Memory triggers. The Divine whispering, "You are returning to yourself."

Then came the symbols in the sky – etched patterns beneath the sun. Symbols similar to Sanskrit, but something I have never seen before. They didn't move like clouds. They hung in place like a sacred language revealing itself. I saw them with my real eyes, and with the eyes behind them. Each one moved diagonally up or down, right to left; it stirred something deep within my cells.

And the colours... they changed too.

I began seeing them not just around people, but everywhere. The imprints of auras, trailing behind movement. The emotions, the thoughts, the heaviness, the purity. It was like watching truth wear a veil of colour.

This was more than awakening.

It was activation.

The dormant strands of DNA – the sacred codes buried beneath generations of distortion – were waking up. It pulsed through my body like electricity and peace at once. I knew it in my bones: I was reactivating what was always mine. Strand by strand, layer by layer, the Divine blueprint reassembled.

I researched obsessively, night after night, chasing crumbs of ancient knowledge and forbidden teachings. I sifted through endless sources – some that sparked recognition, and many that left a bitter taste. There were so many half-truths. Pieces of the puzzle warped just enough to lead people astray.

I saw red flags in spiritual teachers claiming authority, channellers inviting strange energies in, light workers echoing scripts that didn't feel right in my soul. My body would tense. My spirit would withdraw.

That's when I stopped outsourcing my knowing. I stopped giving my power to anyone outside of my own eternal spark.

My intuition became my compass. My body became my truth-teller. My resonance became my guide.

And when I did that, the real remembering began.

I remembered the crystalline city I once called home.

A city of light – alive, humming, iridescent. Towers that glowed with consciousness. Water that remembered your essence. I remember walking barefoot on crystalline floors that sang beneath every step. The air was music. The energy was unity. No deceit. No death. No hierarchy.

It was before the hijack.

Before the fall.

Before the matrix.

And it was real. Not imagination. Memory.

I lived there. I loved there.

And when I remembered, something deep within me broke open. A grief I didn't know I'd been carrying poured out –

grief for what was lost, and joy for what I was becoming again.

I am not this name.

Not this body.

Not these stories.

I am source, encoded in form.

Not in arrogance – but in remembrance. My power was never something I had to earn. It was always mine. Hidden beneath lifetimes of programming, buried under shame, silence and soul amnesia. But no longer.

The light codes, the symbols, the auras, the crystalline city – they weren't visions. They were truth breaking through the veil.

I remembered why they tried to break me. Why they tried to torment me. Why they feared my becoming. Because a woman who sees beyond the veil, who activates the truth in her very blood, who walks with memories of a world uncorrupted by lies – is untouchable. They don't know what to do with that. I am not a pawn, nor a queen, nor even a player in their game anymore. I am the flame that dissolves the board. The cosmic breath that speaks life into dead things. The mother and the storm. And when I walk, I carry every child still trapped in the matrix with me. I carry every version of me that forgot. I carry every soul aching to remember. Because my remembrance is not just for me – it's for the world. This CHAPTER of my becoming is not about power as the world sees it. It is about Divine embodiment.

Sacred memory.

DNA awakening.

Truth-led discernment.

The reclaiming of what was never truly lost. I see now – my power isn't what I can do. It's in who I am. And who I am... was never meant to be small.

CHAPTER THIRTEEN

The Lion's Roar

There comes a time in every warrior's path when silence becomes betrayal. When to hold back truth is to let the chains tighten around the innocent's neck. I reached the threshold when I could no longer bear the quiet suffering I saw around me – souls asleep, eyes glazed with illusion, just programmed, hearts aching but unaware of why. The system or the construct thrives on that slumber. It feeds off confusion, division and fear. But I had remembered, and I felt the power behind who and what we are and I could not keep it inside. I spoke gently at first, to friends, to family, anyone willing to listen. Dropping seeds. Asking questions. I watched their eyes widen, some with interest, some with terror. Most turned away. But a few – ah, a few sparked. I saw it. The flicker of recognition of the truth buried deep. That was enough. It was never about numbers. It was about frequency.

I started writing. Speaking. Whispering light where I could. I used everything I had – my pain, my healing, my journey – as a beacon. I wasn't polished. I was far from perfect, but I was real. And realness is the sword that slices through illusion. The system trembles when even one soul stands fully present in their truth, without fear of being seen. And I had become that. Embodied it. The lion no longer crouched. I stood, mane blazing, eyes fierce with love and justice.

And yet the lion is not always roaring; sometimes it waits in silence, with golden eyes watching the dark.

I am the lion.

It made its way to my back.

And then to my skin. And this is my roar.

CHAPTER FOURTEEN

The Lioness and Her Cubs

There is a primal power in a mother's roar. It doesn't come from rage. It comes from love. The closest love to source. A love so fierce, it would tear through dimensions to protect what is hers.

When I awakened to the Divine Feminine, I saw clearly what I had always known in my soul: I was never just a woman. I was a protector. A shield. A force the darkness feared. And I had three reasons to become indestructible, just as the lioness protects her cubs.

They say motherhood makes you soft. Maybe for some. But for me, it sharpened my instincts. Every scar I bore became armour. Every wound became a vow. My children did not just inherit my blood – they inherited my strength. And I vowed they would never suffer as I did. Not under my watch.

My first cub sees the world in sharp contrast – black or white, truth or lie. He senses when something isn't right. He is quiet, observant and unshakably loyal.

My second cub has the softest heart and the fiercest spirit, carrying an inner light that glows through even the darkest days.

And my last cub – my daughter – carries the fire in her eyes, the same one I saw in my dreams. A flame of remembrance.

People tried to break me for years. Abusers. Institutions. Voices that whispered I was crazy. Voices that screamed I was too much. I was told to sit down, shut up, take the pills, fit in and play small.

And something rose within me. And it said: "NO."

I had endured too much to let my children grow up thinking that silence is strength. That suffering in secret is noble. That survival is enough. No. I will show them what thriving looks like. What being sovereign in a broken world feels like.

I don't want them to fear darkness. I want them to transmute it. Just as I have. I want them to know that pain can become purpose. That trauma can become a torch. And that love – real, sacred, source-given love – can make a lion out of anyone.

Some people still see me and whisper:

"She's intense."

Damn right, I am.

Because when you're raising lions,

you don't get to be a house cat.

CHAPTER FIFTEEN

The Rise of the Divine Feminine

She was always there.

They never taught me what the Divine Feminine truly was. They dressed her up in lace and told me she was gentle, submissive, soft. But they lied.

The Divine Feminine I came to know? She's a wildfire. She's the scream that shatters silence. She's the mother bear who will destroy everything that threatens her children.

She is the blood.

She is the birth.

She is death and resurrection.

I didn't meet her through ceremony or sacred circles. I met her in my pain. I met her in the bruises I covered up, in the nights I prayed no one would find me. She rose every time I was knocked down. She rose when I stood in courtrooms alone. She rose when I told people the truth no one wanted to hear.

She didn't come to save me. She came to remind me that I didn't need saving.

That I was the sword.

That I was the storm.

You can't silence what was born of fire. You can't tame what was made from stardust and bone.

For years, they broke me. But every scar became a map – a path back to her. Back to me.

I am the Divine Feminine. Not because I am perfect. But because I survived what was meant to destroy me. And I didn't just survive – I remembered.

I remembered who I was before the world told me who to be. Before I was moulded, silenced, used. Before I was blamed, broken and betrayed.

I remember the primal, ancient knowing in my womb. The softness that holds galaxies, and the rage that shakes kingdoms. They may fear her. They may hate her. But she will rise anyway. Through every truth that was buried. She rises in me. And she will never go back to sleep.

CHAPTER SIXTEEN

In the Beginning... was the Lie

I used to believe the story that there was a god in the sky who made the world and ruled over everything. That pain was part of some Divine plan. That suffering was for our growth, our evolution. That if we just had faith, obeyed and stayed humble, we would be rewarded.

But none of that ever felt right. Why would a loving creator allow children to be abused?

Why would a true god need to be worshipped, feared, or obeyed?

It wasn't until I hit rock bottom — after a spiritual attack, after darkness clawed at the edges of my life — that I asked the real question: Who built this world? Because it sure as hell didn't feel like love.

The hijacking of creation.

This reality... is a copy. A mirror of something Divine — but twisted. It looks real. It feels real. But it's tampered with.

The original world — the true earth was created in alignment with Source. Balanced. Beautiful. Alive.

But it was hijacked.

Some call it the demiurge.

Others say Enlil, Yaldabaoth. Names don't matter.

What matters is it wasn't Source.

Something was feeding off us, and nobody was saying it.

The truth about Sophia, a name very few know. I didn't know her at first; I felt her. That ache in my chest knowing that the Divine mother was missing- The feminine aspect of source, The cosmic mother, the real representation of wisdom. Erased from religion, and the structure of reality.

Sophia isn't a goddess. She's the original blueprint of creation. She tried to bring life into form – but her energy was used, twisted by the false light creator to build this trap. She fell... and so did we.

That's why everything sacred was flipped. That's why women were silenced, magic was demonised and children were broken. Because if the Divine Mother ever rose again, the whole system would collapse. And that's what's happening now.

CHAPTER SEVENTEEN

The Matrix – A Construct, Not Creation

You don't need to be a philosopher or a mystic to realise something is off about the world we know today. We were born into a system we didn't choose and from the moment we arrive, it begins shaping us. Programming. Brainwashing. Quietly. Consistently. Completely.

This system has a name.

The Matrix.

Not just the movie – but a real, spiritual, psychological and energetic construct designed to keep you distracted, disempowered and disconnected from your truth.

The Matrix is a control system. It's not just physical – it's mental, emotional, social and spiritual. Its purpose? To keep you feeding it with your energy... while believing you are free. It starts programming you when you're born; you're told who to be. Good girl, be quiet, don't question. You're measured by grades, Obedience, appearance. You're told success is money, status, validation. The matrix thrives on noise and endless stimulation. Distraction loops, scrolling endlessly. Shopping, comparing, consuming, constant drama and division. All of it keeps you from turning inward – where your true power lives. Emotional hijacking, your emotions are currency. Fear. Anger. Guilt. Shame – they feed the system. The news is engineered to trigger fear. Social media fuels inadequacy and comparison. You're taught to suppress or overreact, but never just to feel and understand. The illusion of choice; you're offered "options" – jobs, politics, beliefs – but all within a limited framework. Left or right. Coke or Pepsi. Religion A or B. The illusion is that you're choosing freely when, in truth, you're choosing between cages. The Matrix doesn't care what side you pick – only that you keep playing the game. And last of all, the energy harvesting; this is where it gets spiritual. Your life force is powerful. Your attention is sacred. But the Matrix siphons your energy through negative thought loops, addiction and trauma, toxic relationships, false light systems. Every time you give energy to fear, shame or illusion – something feeds.

Call it the Demiurge, the Archons, or simply the system – the force behind the Matrix isn't just human corruption. Its energetic intelligence that feeds on disconnection and control.

It doesn't want you dead.

It wants you distracted.

Alive – but asleep.

Because an awakened soul is unpredictable. Non-programmable and Sovereign.

CHAPTER EIGHTEEN

The Reincarnation Trap – A Beautiful Lie

I used to believe I chose this life. That my soul picked this pain, that I agreed to trauma before I got here. But tell me – what kind of soul would willingly choose to be abused, starved, enslaved?

That belief was a program. A spiritual gaslight wrapped in pretty words like "soul contract," "karma" and "lessons," keep people passive. It keeps them from fighting back. It teaches them to accept evil as if they deserve it. But here's the truth I've come to live and know. When a soul dies here, it doesn't float off into Divine peace.

It's intercepted,

drawn towards a tunnel of light

filled with fake "guides", ascended masters", or "family", encouraging you to review your life. But what you're shown isn't truth. It's edited, filtered, made to trigger guilt or shame.

So, you "choose" to try again.

Back into another life.

Back into more trauma.

Back into another machine.

It's not reincarnation. It's recycling.

CHAPTER NINETEEN

The Great Forgetting

Once, we danced between stars – sovereign, luminous, multidimensional. We were creators, not prisoners. Free to roam worlds, slip between dimensions, birth galaxies from thought and feel only what we chose to feel.

But that story was stolen.

Our truth was veiled.

Somewhere, long ago – or perhaps not long at all – we were lured here. Whispered into illusion. Not by Source. Not by the true light, but by a mimic. A false light. A siren call, wrapped in beauty and curiosity:

"Come and see what it's like to forget, to be human, to experience limitations. It's just a game. You can leave any time."

We believed it.

And that was the trick.

When we entered, we fell. Not in sin – but in density. The veil closed behind us. Memory wiped. Abilities locked. Sovereignty buried under programs and systems designed to keep us asleep. This earth... was not the garden it was meant to be. It was a trap.

A soul farm.

An experiment turned into a prison, wrapped in false light and reincarnation loops. They made us forget so we wouldn't try to escape. They made us small so we wouldn't remember how big we are.

But even here... something never died.

They can cloak the sky.

They can warp the history.

But they cannot erase what we carry in our hearts.

This is not a New Age love and light.

This is a jailbreak.

The truth doesn't feel pretty. It burns.

It shatters illusions but also sets you free.

I remembered. And now, so will you.

CHAPTER TWENTY

The Override Codes

Before coming in, some souls – old ones, rebels, protectors – placed something inside themselves.

A key.

A seed.

A code that could not be deleted.

It lived in our DNA, buried under trauma, bloodlines and distractions.

It waited in the dark.

Until we were ready.

And when the time came... when the pain cracked us open just enough... when the illusion became too thin to believe anymore...

The override code was activated.

It may have looked like a breakdown. Or a sudden knowing. A dream, a flash, a moment you couldn't explain.

Something inside you refused to obey the lie any longer.

That was your soul remembering itself.

That was the override.

It cannot be given to you. It cannot be forced. It awakens

the moment you choose to remember – and never again allow yourself to be silenced, sold or steered. You begin to see. To feel the bars of the invisible cage. And more importantly – you begin to slip through them. Not everyone around you will understand. They may call it madness. But what they call madness is actually freedom.

And once your override code is active, you will start to see it in others too. The glint in the eye. The truth in their words. The subtle rebellion in their energy. We had to forget in order to remember, but now we are remembering in order to return.

CHAPTER TWENTY ONE

The Final Exit

They built a trap that mimics light. A tunnel. A voice. A feeling of peace. But it's the ultimate deception cloaked in comfort – an ancient recycling system. It doesn't free you. It resets you.

This is the trap at death – the false light memory wipes the agreements you don't remember signing. The Matrix doesn't end with the physical world. It follows the soul into the afterlife.

When the time comes to leave this body, stay calm.

No fear. No rushing. No following anything blindly.

You're not a lost soul. You are not confused. You are eternal, and you get to choose.

If you see a tunnel of light or familiar faces, pause. Breathe. Feel it. Don't react, respond from your deepest truth.

Ask yourself: Does this feel like love, or does it feel like a lure? Real truth doesn't pull you. It opens up from within.

Remember who you are. Stand firm. You don't need to go anywhere unless you feel the resonance of your own source within it. Say it clearly, "I am sovereign. I do not consent to recycling, contracts, or false light. I return to source on my own authority."

Then wait. Let the noise fade. Let the illusion dissolve.

You will feel the difference. Real peace doesn't demand. It doesn't coax. It simply is.

When that feeling rises from within you, like remembering instead of being told, follow it. That's the exit.

Not the flashiest one. Not the loudest. But the true one.

You came here with that code inside you. And when the moment comes, you will know. Because freedom doesn't feel like surrender. It feels like home.

And then what?

You don't just escape.

You regain your birthright.

Freedom to explore infinite dimensions.

Power to create clean realities.

Communion with source – no hierarchy.

Clarity that can never be stolen.

You are not absorbed. You are not recycled. You are restored.

You can also still protect the ones you love.

Once free, you don't forget those you left behind. You become a quiet guardian. A true protector – not stuck in a wheel, but outside it, holding a torch. You can:

Send them strength without words.

Shield them from energetic interference.

Leave them seeds of remembrance.

Guide them silently when their moment comes. Your love doesn't die; it amplifies- Because now it is clean.

CHAPTER TWENTY-TWO

Heaven was Never Far

After I broke the override codes – after I cut the contracts, cleared the false guides and stood fully in my sovereignty – I expected more chaos.

But it didn't come.

For the first time in my life, things started to feel simple.

I wasn't fighting invisible battles every night.

I wasn't waiting for the next attack. I wasn't trying to explain my truth to people who weren't ready.

There was just… space,

A deep quiet in my body that I had never known. I woke up one morning and noticed the sunlight coming through the blinds. I didn't just see it – I felt it. That used to be rare. I was always too tired or too on edge to feel anything like peace.

But now?

I had energy again.

I could laugh with my kids without that weight on my chest. I could sit outside and just be, without trying to solve something or protect against something.

I looked at my home – the one I renovated – and for the first time, it felt like mine.

Safe.

Sacred.

Like heaven wasn't above me, but all around me. The real sign that something had shifted was I didn't need to explain myself anymore. I didn't care who believed me. That need dissolved. I stopped looking for signs every day. I didn't feel like I needed to chase proof of the Divine. I just knew. My children seemed calmer. The energy in our house changed: less tension more flow. I stopped reacting out of fear. Situations that would've overwhelmed me before, now felt easy to handle.

I realised... maybe this is what "heaven" always meant. Not some perfect place. Just the moment you finally feel safe in your body, safe in your truth, safe in your own home. Heaven was never far. It was just buried under the noise. And now the noise is gone, I will never let it in again.

Peace doesn't mean nothing happens. It means nothing owns you.

CHAPTER TWENTY-THREE

The Truth Hidden in the Dark

For most of my life, I believed the darkness was out to get me.

And maybe, for a time, it was. It crept in through the cracks.

It whispered lies when I was weak.

It tried to break me, scare me, consume me.

I spent years fighting it, running, surviving, praying it would leave me alone.

And every time I thought I'd escaped it, it came back with a new face, a new test. But here's what I finally understood;

The darkness didn't come to destroy me.

It came to show me who I am.

It revealed everything I still feared. It dragged up every unhealed part of me. It shattered every illusion I clung to.

And when I stopped fighting it, when I stood in the middle of it and said, "I'm not afraid anymore," it bowed.

Because the real darkness. The primordial void. Was never my enemy.

It was the womb of my becoming. It didn't want to kill me. It wanted me to remember.

To remember that I am not hunted. I am the fire. I am the sovereign soul who walked through Hell and made it sacred.

What once tormented me, became my teacher.

What once felt like death, was actually rebirth.

Now I see that the false light wanted me weak.

But the darkness made me unshakable.

So, if you've been haunted, hunted, or brought to your knees, this is your reminder.

You weren't being destroyed, you were being forged.

The darkness doesn't mean you're lost; it means you're on the edge of remembering.

And if you've made it to this page, it wasn't by accident. Your soul guided you here to remember what I remembered in the fire.

You are the key.

You hold the true light.

And you were never meant to stay small.

Now rise.

CHAPTER TWENTY-FOUR

The Mirror and the Flame

There is a silence that only comes after the storm, a peace not born of comfort, but of confrontation. It is not gifted. It is earned.

I thought for a long time that the darkness was my enemy. That the torment I had endured, the attacks I faced, the fear that clawed at my skin… were forces outside of me. And many of them were. But the real reckoning didn't happen when I pushed them away; it happened when I turned inward. When I finally stopped running and instead, looked in the mirror.

There I met someone I had been avoiding my whole life, myself.

Not the self I showed the world, not the self I tried to fix, but the raw, trembling, powerful essences underneath it all. The one who carried every memory, every wound every suppressed scream. I looked into her eyes and I didn't look away.

That was the scariest thing I've done. Not fighting entities. Not breaking free from illusions. But facing myself.

And yet… it was in that moment that everything changed.

Because when I met myself in the dark, like *really* met myself, I found the darkness wasn't empty; it was full. Full of fragments I had abandoned. Full of truths I wasn't ready to face. Full of light that had been covered in ash.

I realised then, the torment was real. But it wasn't just punishment. It was preparation. Every shadow I faced was a doorway. Every fear, a forgotten part of me asking to come home.

I walked through each one, bleeding but brave. And on the other side of that journey… was peace.

Not the kind of peace people talk about lightly. But the kind that settles in your bones. The kind that knows you can never be broken again because you met the part of you that can never die.

And now, I no longer fear the darkness. I no longer fear myself.

I no longer flinch when a new shadow arises.

I smile.

Because I know what's waiting inside it, another key, another truth, another piece of me.

The light I carry now isn't one that avoids the dark. It was forged in it. It knows the dark. And it stands tall and no longer hides.

I am whole.

I am the storm and the stillness.

I am the mirror and the flame.

And from this place of peace, I can finally say,

I am free.

CHAPTER TWENTY-FIVE

Final Prayer

May the truth that stirred within you, never be silenced.

May your light rise sovereign, fierce and unshakable.

May the chains of illusion fall away with grace

and every shadow that once haunted you, now bow to your strength.

I call upon the eternal flame of Source to illuminate your path.

I ask that your soul be shielded in Divine protection,

that remembrance floods your being in waves of knowing,

and that you walk forward – awake, aware and free.

You are not alone.

You were never broken,

you were always the key.

And so, I ask you now,

when the veil thins

and the false light calls,

what will you choose?

Will you remember?

Let this be a reminder, you were born of love,

wrapped in strength and destined to rise.

www.ingramcontent.com/pod-product-compliance
Lightning Source LLC
Chambersburg PA
CBHW071222070526
44584CB00019B/3116